"Poetry Galore & More with Shel Silverstein"

Cheryl Potts

Published by Alleyside Press, a Division of Upstart, Inc.
P. O. Box 889
Hagerstown, MD 21741

ISBN 0-913853-34-8

Printed in the United States of America

Acknowledgments

Thanks to Bill Higby, our art teacher, for giving me
permission to use his illustrations.

Thanks also to my colleagues, for the encouragement
to make this workshop into a book.

Contents

Introduction

Each school year, elementary teachers are bombarded with a new set of challenges! Now more than ever, we have become self-esteem builders, motivators and at times attitude-changers of children. There's always a demand for more creative ideas and enthusiasm-building activities to keep our students on task. We are constantly teaching our students how to be "life-long learners."

Poetry Galore and More with Shel Silverstein was created for the elementary teacher who likes to interact and become involved in the learning process of his or her students. The book was designed to create an enthusiasm and excitement in poetry and literature, as well as reinforce many basic reading/writing skills. It encompasses a wide assortment of language arts and reading ideas, discussions, mini-lessons, games, projects, and activities using the following Shel Silverstein books: *Where the Sidewalk Ends; A Light in the Attic; The Missing Piece; The Missing Piece Meets the Big O; Lafcadio, the Lion Who Shot Back; The Giving Tree; Who Wants a Cheap Rhinoceros?;* and *A Giraffe and a Half.* His poems create springboards for many classroom activities, because they don't always end happily or the way you'd expect them to. That's part of what makes Shel Silverstein uniquely creative and consistently enjoyable for young audiences.

This book is more than an author study, though. It is meant to replace "worksheet mania" with hands-on activities and projects the children will not only enjoy but learn from as well. These activities can, at any time, be inserted into your regular or whole language program, year after year, to fit the needs and learning styles of your students.

The construction of homemade games can be an exciting and motivating tool in your classroom. If you keep the following suggestions in mind, your chances of making games that are valuable will be greatly increased:

1. Games should only be used to reinforce skills and concepts that have already been introduced.

2. Games should be chosen and made so they are durable, practical, and worth your time making them. (Use contact paper and/or laminating film where possible.) After each use, the activities materials (including small parts, tape recordings, etc.) may be placed in a string-tied manila envelope with a copy of the poem(s) attached to the envelope for easy retrieval.

3. Successful games are usually simple, short, repetitive, and fun.

4. Wherever appropriate, teacher-made games should be self-correcting.

5. Whenever possible, involve the students in helping you make classroom games. They can save you time and will feel more ownership and responsibility toward the care of them.

6. Games can be used by individuals, in small groups, or in large groups; competitively or cooperatively; for demonstration, as an assigned time filler, and as a teacher observation of students' progress.

In addition to the games, activities, and projects described throughout this book, there are also many other ways to help students enjoy and benefit from exposure to Shel Silverstein's talent and creativity:

1. Students may wish to select their favorite poem and record it on a cassette tape.

2. Students may want to select a poem, memorize it, and recite it for the class, using lots of expression.

3. Students may decide to write their own poetry, illustrating themselves or cutting pictures from magazines to go along with it.

4. Students may want to compile poems from various sources by choosing a topic or theme (such as holidays, cats and dogs, summer, etc.). This could be used for a parent gift or as an addition to the classroom library.

5. You, as the teacher, may wish to incorporate a "poetry pause" during the school day, sharing and acting out a poem to entertain, surprise, or motivate your students.

6. With help, students may be able to put their poems or someone else's to music, using a familiar children's song.

7. Students may like to illustrate Shel Silverstein's poems that he did not illustrate.

8. Different types of poetry may be introduced at this time for students to experiment with or compare to Silverstein's.

9. Students may wish to vote on their best-liked poems from Silverstein's books.

10. Students can compare the styles of two or more famous children's poets, such as Shel Silverstein, Jack Prelutsky, and Jeff Moss.

11. Students can keep a poetry journal for the school year, collecting their favorites and/or writing their own.

12. Students may wish to use objects, pictures, or other aids to enhance their telling of a poem to the class.

13. Students may enjoy playing "poetry charade" by acting out the title of a familiar poem for classmates to guess.

14. A tree branch secured in a planter and decorated with poem apples, leaves, birds, snowflakes, etc. (pertinent to seasonal changes), can create a fun incentive for a child to pick and read a poem each day.

Part One

Where the Sidewalk Ends

Activity 1: Oral Reading/Comprehension

Poems:

"The Acrobats," page 10
"Afraid of the Dark," page 159
"Homemade Boat," page 12
"I Must Remember," page 14
"Invisible Boy," page 82
"It's Dark in Here," page 21
"Pancake?" page 34
"Tree House," page 79

These poems can be enlarged and mounted on poster board for easier use in the classroom. When you introduce a poem, display it on an easel and have several students take turns reading aloud. This, then, can become the poem of the day. The following pages contain poem question sheets that students may fill in or that you may use for comprehension exercises (orally or for a quick evaluation of comprehending skills). Regardless, by the end of the unit, you'll be surprised how involved students become in reading poems to their classmates, parents, and anyone who will listen! The real key is your enthusiasm as the teacher. Above all, keep the reading and studying of poetry as nonthreatening and fun as possible. This will give your students a positive experience to carry with them into high school, when they study poetry more seriously.

Name_____   Date_____

"The Acrobats"

1. What is this poem all about? _____

   _____

2. What words rhyme with *knees?* _____

   _____

3. What does *acrobat* mean? _____

   _____

4. Why shouldn't the top acrobat sneeze?_____

   _____

Name_____   Date_____

"Afraid of the Dark"

1. What is Reginald Clark afraid of?_____

   _____

2. What does Reginald need to do before he can settle down? _____

   _____

3. What things seem to comfort him? _____

   _____

4. Why does Reginald say, "Please do not close this book on me?"____

   _____

Name_____   Date_____

"Homemade Boat"

1. What is the main idea of this poem? _____

_____

2. What does *divine* mean? _____

_____

3. What materials would be needed to build a boat?_____

_____

4. What part(s) of a boat would be the most important? _____

_____

Name_____   Date_____

"I Must Remember"

1. What is this poem all about? _____

_____

2. What does *dunce* mean? _____

_____

3.What food do we eat on Sunday? _____

_____

4.Leftovers are for what day of the week? _____

_____

Name_____   Date_____

"Invisible Boy"

1. What is the main idea of this poem? _____

    _____

2. What does an invisible boy look like?_____

    _____

3. Is this "a beautiful picture to see"? _____

    _____

4. Can you draw an invisible picture? _____

    _____

Name_____   Date_____

"It's Dark in Here"

1. What is this poem about? _____

    _____

2. Why is the speaker inside the lion's mouth? _____

    _____

3. What words rhyme with *here?* _____

    _____

4. What is the speaker writing? _____

    _____

"Pancake?"

1. What is the main idea of this poem? _____

   _____

2. Who wants a pancake? _____

   _____

3. What word rhymes with *griddle?* _____

   _____

4. What words describe Grace and Theresa?_____

   _____

"Tree House"

1. What is this poem about? _____

   _____ _____

2. What words describe the tree house? _____

   _____

3. What other kind of house does the speaker describe?_____

   _____

4. What does "cozy" mean? _____

   _____

Activity 2: Opposites

Poem:

"Band-aids," page 140

After reading the poem, make a large poster of a boy with sores, cuts, and bruises all over the upper part of his body. On each "boo-boo" write a word that has an opposite. Write the opposite words on large Band-Aids (one each) to match up with the words on the large poster. Put a piece of low-tack tape on the back of each Band-Aid so that they'll be reusable game pieces.

This game may be played with a small group or as an independent activity when students are finished with other assignments. To play, a leader passes out the Band-Aids to players. In turn, each child goes to the poster and matches his or her Band-Aid to the "boo-boo" with the correct opposite word. Corrections may be made while students play the game or after the "boo-boos" are all covered, then the children may take turns "pulling" off the Band-Aids and checking answers.

As an alternative activity, children may enjoy writing rhyming stories using their own names as the main character. Guide your students in making a list of words that rhyme with their name. Children may want to use a nickname or shortened version of their name to make rhyming easier. Even nonsense words are acceptable, for example:

Bill, hill, still, chill, pill, fill, drill, mill, etc.

Sue, glue, shoe, flu, stew, new, chew, crew, blue, etc.

Mindy, bow-bindy, floppy-flindy, tindy, go-indy, etc.

Mike, spike, hike, bike, like, pike, yike, etc.

Ask children to create a silly story using these rhyming words at the end of each line. Be prepared to give suggestions, but keep it fun! Here's an example:

There once was a boy named Shawn,

who woke up one morning with a yawn.

He looked out on the lawn

and saw a cute fawn.

But when he got to the door, it was gone.

Encourage your children to illustrate their story and make it into a book. Your students may enjoy reading some rhyming stories such as *Ten Loopy Caterpillars* by (Joy Cowley), *On Sunday I Lost My Cat* (by Jan Demurs), *"I Can't" Said the Ant* (by Polly Cameron), *Chicken Soup With Rice* (by Maurice Sendak), and *Drummer Hoff* (by Barbara Emberley).

Activity 3: Rhyming

Poem:

"Sarah Cynthia Sylvia Stout," pages 70–71

After reading aloud or listening to Shel Silverstein sing this poem, have students try the "Garbage Game." Make a game board with a START space in each corner. Down each side of the board draw eight spaces with a rhymable word in each. Give each of four players a marker or game piece to put on his or her own START space. In order to move along the game board, players throw a piece of "garbage" (a big wad of paper) into a wastebasket three or more feet away. If the player successfully gets the garbage into the wastebasket, he or she earns one move on the game board and has to produce a word that will rhyme with the word landed on, not duplicating others' words. If the player misses the throw into the wastebasket, he or she forfeits the turn. Play continues until one player successfully moves through all eight spaces on his or her side of the game board.

START	jump	dog	side	meat	do	how	so	fun	START
brown									face
now									miss
this			Place copy of						door
star			poem in here						hair
fair									that
name									pot
box									bed
stuff									hook
START	train	week	not	flow	rest	play	stop	chin	START

Activity 4: True/False/Opinion

Poem:

"The Crocodile's Toothache," page 66

After reading the poem, this game can follow. To make, use a three-slotted shoe box or three empty cans with plastic covers and a slit cut in the top of each. Mark each shoe-box slot or can with *True, False,* or *Opinion.* Cut several 3x5 index cards in half and write one statement on each card. If you want this game to be self-correcting, code the back of each card.

This game may be played in a small group or as an independent activity. Sample statements and answers for each card are listed below:

1. You need to go to college to become a dentist. (T)
2. There are a lot of dentists in our area. (O)
3. Dentists may take X rays of your teeth (T)
4. Dentists can fill your cavities. (T)
5. Dentists themselves always have nice teeth. (F)
6. Dentists have very big offices. (O)
7. Crocodiles can open their jaws wide. (T)
8. Everyone gets a second set of teeth. (T)
9. You need to brush your teeth every day. (T)
10. Dentists hurt people. (O)
11. Dentists are nice people. (O)
12. Dentists pull out whatever teeth they want to. (F)
13. Some people have false teeth. (T)
14. A crocodile can floss its teeth. (F)
15. Children lose their teeth. (T)
16. Crocodiles brush their teeth. (F)
17. Crocodiles wear braces. (F)
18. Crocodiles live in our area. (T,F)
19. Crocodiles are reptiles. (T)
20. Crocodiles make good pets. (O)
21. Eating candy is good for your teeth. (F)
22. Crocodiles eat dentists. (F)
23. Crocodiles' teeth are sharp. (T)
24. Crocodiles don't need their teeth. (F)
25. You should go to the dentist every six months. (T)

To play this game in a small group setting, deal out all of the statement cards to the players. Each player, in turn, reads a card and places it in the appropriate slot. Students may discuss the best answer. When the cards have all been placed, the game is over and students can check each statement card for the appropriate code. The incorrectly placed cards may be discussed.

Activity 5a: Brainstorming

Poem:

"Jimmy Jet and His TV Set," pages 28–29

Read the poem and initiate a discussion of what other activities can replace TV watching. Let students brainstorm and share the activities and hobbies that they enjoy. List their ideas on poster paper, then hang it where students can add to it at any time. From this list let your students choose to illustrate one or more of these "non-TV activities." Put all of the illustrations together into a classroom book entitled, *Turned Off. . . Tuned In: Things to Do That are more interesting than watching TV.*

This would also be a good time to read the poem "Channels" from *A Light in the Attic.*

Activity 5b: Keeping a Journal

Another approach involves the parents in a little experiment! Send home a letter to your students' parents stating something similar to this:

Dear Parents:

Our class has designated next week as "TV-withdrawal week." Students will quit watching TV "cold turkey" for one week, replacing it with other meaningful and creative activities. These alternative activities should be listed in a journal and handed in as your child's report the first day of the following week. Please encourage your child to participate in this important experiment.

Sincerely,

Journal Entry

Name_____   Date/Time_____

Description of non-TV activity:

_____
Parent Signature

Activity 5c: Letter Writing

On the other hand, students may wish to be "TV critics." Encourage them to be honest and specific as they critique various TV programs. Take it a step further and suggest that they write to the networks, local stations, the F.C.C., and even the advertisers with their opinion of the quality of the programming. Participants can write to their local station directly or "in care of" the network's address:

ABC Television
7 Lincoln Square
New York, NY 10019

CBS Television
Programming Dept.
555 West 57th St.
New York, NY 10019

NBC Television
30 Rockefeller Plaza
New York, NY 10019

F.C.C.
1919 M St. N.W.
Washington, DC 20554

"TV Critic"

Name of program _____

Date seen_____Station or channel _____

City_____State_____ ZIP_____

I am writing to you because . . .

I would like to suggest . . .

Signed_____

If students wish to include their name and address, have them *print* the information.

Activity 6: Alphabetical Order

Poem:
"Sick," pages 58–59

Read the poem, then review the names of the body parts that Silverstein mentions. Turn this into an alphabetical order game by listing the names on a teacher-made sheet for the students to cut apart. Students may want to draw a simple illustration on each card. Using a 3-minute egg-timer, children can work together or individually to see how quickly they can put the word cards in alphabetical order.

For a more competitive game, make two sets of word cards, one yellow and one white, and give two players one set each. The players first put their sets of cards face down in front of them. At the same time, each player turns over the top card and decides which word would be listed first in the dictionary. The player who says the word first takes both cards and places them into his or her "winnings" pile. If the players each turn up a card with the same word, they turn over their next card and play continues. The player with the most cards collected when the decks are exhausted is the winner.

The poem "Kidnapped" from *A Light in the Attic* also ties in with this topic. This is a good time to lead a discussion on exaggeration, tall tales, real versus make believe, and honesty. You might use additional books such as *Pecos Bill, Paul Bunyan* (by Steven Kellogg), *Mike Fink* (by Carol Beach York), and others.

appendix	elbow	tongue
brain	hip	hair
throat	heart	leg
chin	bellybutton	mouth
tonsils	ankle	back
ear	thumb	toes
	nose	

Activity 7: Creative Writing

Poem:

"The Silver Fish," page 148

Make a large poster of a child fishing off a riverbank. Attach a piece of yarn to the end of the pole, and tie a safety pin to the bottom of the yarn. Cover a cardboard fish cutout with aluminum foil to look like the fish in the poem. Attach the fish to the safety pin and secure the poster to a bulletin board. After reading the poem with your class, brainstorm ways in which students would use up "their wishes" if they had caught the silver fish. Encourage the children to write their own version of the story. The poster will serve as a visual to help students generate ideas as well as the central decoration for their display of finished stories.

Your students may wish to write a holiday variation of this story by changing the characters. For instance, the story may be of an old man who goes into the forest and catches a leprechaun (for St. Patrick's Day) or a child who catches a wild turkey in the woods (for a Thanksgiving Day story).

As a follow-up activity, have each child make and cut out a fish, and then select or write a poem to glue on the back of each. Attach a paper clip or a piece of magnetic tape to the mouth of the fish. Using a small pool and a homemade fishing pole with a magnet as the "hook," have children put all of their fish into the "pond" and take turns catching a fish and reading a poem.

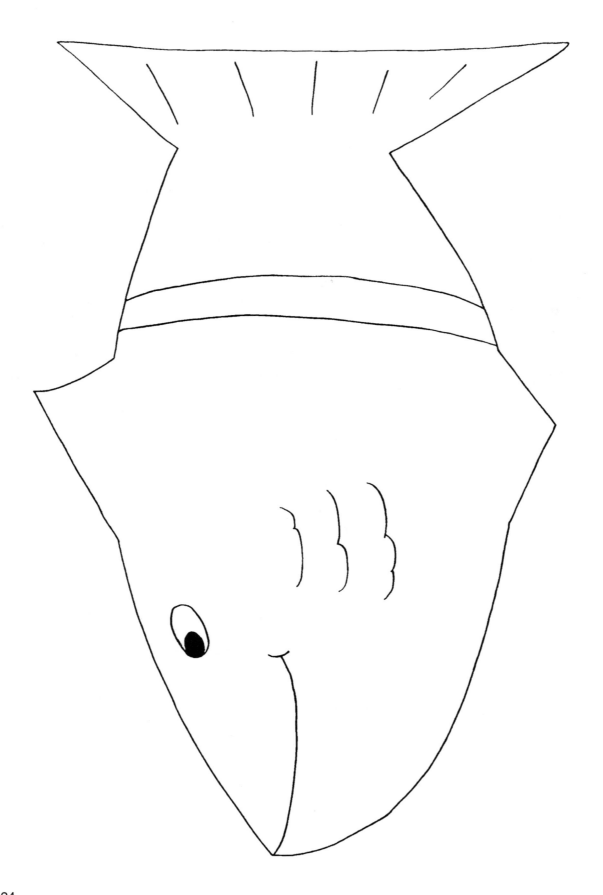

Activity 8: Role-playing/Sequencing

Poem:

"Smart," page 35

After reading the poem together as a class, ask for volunteers to role-play the poem's characters and discover for themselves the mistakes the boy made. The characters in order of appearance are Dad, the speaker, the unknown swapper, Lou, old blind Bates, and Hiram Coombs. Encourage the children to use facial expressions, body language, and some dialogue to make the poem come alive. Ask them, "Why did Dad get red in the cheeks, close his eyes, and shake his head when his son showed him the money he got back?" Discuss Dad's body language and how it might indicate to his son whether he did the right thing or not.

Since there is no illustration of this poem in Shel Silverstein's book, have the children use their imaginations to draw a picture of the little boy and his father. As a review of the poem sequence, have the children fold a paper into sixths and draw the events of the poem in order. Divide your classroom into groups of four, requesting that the students retell the story to a partner.

This poem may also be a wonderful introduction to a math unit on money and making change.

Activity 9: Spelling/Abbreviations

Poem:

"Flag," page 24

Abbreviations are used widely in all kinds of reading materials, saving time, space, and writing energy.

Although the poem "Flag" is short, it can serve as an introduction to a unit on the spelling and abbreviations of America's 50 states. Students may find it easier to memorize the states in alphabetical order first, then learn the abbreviations. To make this activity more fun, there is a song titled: "50 States in Rhyme" by Phil and Lynn Brower, available on audio cassette from Benson Music Group, Inc. (365 Great Circle Rd., Nashville, TN 37228). The 50 states in alphabetical order with their abbreviations follow:

Alabama	AL	Montana	MT
Alaska	AK	Nebraska	NE
Arizona	AZ	Nevada	NV
Arkansas	AR	New Hampshire	NH
California	CA	New Jersey	NJ
Colorado	CO	New Mexico	NM
Connecticut	CT	New York	NY
Delaware	DE	North Carolina	NC
Florida	FL	North Dakota	ND
Georgia	GA	Ohio	OH
Hawaii	HI	Oklahoma	OK
Idaho	ID	Oregon	OR
Illinois	IL	Pennsylvania	PA
Indiana	IN	Rhode Island	RI
Iowa	IA	South Carolina	SC
Kansas	KS	South Dakota	SD
Kentucky	KY	Tennessee	TN
Louisiana	LA	Texas	TX
Maine	ME	Utah	UT
Maryland	MD	Vermont	VT
Massachusetts	MA	Virginia	VA
Michigan	MI	Washington	WA
Minnesota	MN	West Virginia	WV
Mississippi	MS	Wisconsin	WI
Missouri	MO	Wyoming	WY

To give students more practice in using abbreviations, make up crossword puzzles, flashcards, or "bubblegrams," or create a competitive activity by encouraging students to memorize abbreviations. To encourage participation in this mental challenge, tell your students that those successfully mastering the task will get their picture featured in the local newspaper.

Other commonly used abbreviations for students to become familiar with are the following:

Ave.	avenue	lb.	pound	Pl.	place
bldg.	building	min.	minute	qt.	quart
dept.	department	Mr.	mister	Rd.	road
Dr.	doctor	Mrs.	mistress	Rt.	route
doz.	dozen	no.	number	sec.	second
gal.	gallon	oz.	ounce	St.	street
govt.	government	pkg.	package	wt.	weight
hr.	hour	pg.	page	yd.	yard
in.	inch	pt.	pint	yr.	year

For a more complete list of abbreviations, refer to *The Reading Teacher's Book of Lists* by Edward Fry, Jacqueline Polk, and Dona Fountoukidis.

The following page presents a bubblegram of abbreviations. Students should use the clues at the bottom of the page and fill in the abbreviations in the bubbles provided. Bubblegrams can be used for many topics of study. Write the topic vertically and use words that refer to your topic, adding the clues at the bottom of your sheet or on an attached page. Encourage your children to create these as a theme wrap-up to see how much vocabulary they learned. Use bubblegrams as a quiz or to review for a test. Check your student-written bubblegrams for accuracy, then hand them out randomly for students to fill in for a homework assignment or a final quiz.

Abbreviation Bubblegram

Using the clues at the bottom of the page, fill in the correctly spelled abbreviations in the bubbles provided.

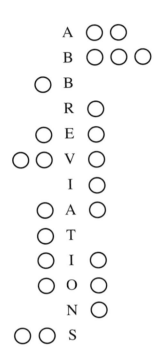

Clues:

A	avenue	A	gallon
B	building	T	street
B	pound	I	minute
R	road	O	dozen
E	second	N	number
V	government	S	mistress
I	inch		

Part Two

A Light in the Attic

Activity 10: Music

Poems:

You can teach your students poems by putting them to familiar children's tunes.

The poem "Arrows" fits with the tune "Rock-a-bye Baby" with one minor word change to the poem. Instead of saying the word "toward" in the first line of the poem, replace it with the word "into."

Sing the poem "Hammock" to the tune of "A Tisket, A-Tasket."

The poem, "Signals" works well to the tune of "If You're Happy and You Know it."

"Examination" fits well with the tune "On Top of Spaghetti."

Try putting the tune "99 Bottles of Beer on the Wall" to the poem "Snap!"

The poem "Overdues" works well with the tune "Three Blind Mice" with a little variation and repetition of the tune on lines 5–8. (The school librarian will enjoy hearing this rendition of Shel Silverstein's poem!)

Try singing the poem "Hitting" to the tune, "Oh, My Darlin', Clementine." Use lines 5 and 6 as a "refrain" in place of "You are lost and gone forever..." Also change the last line of the poem to read: Use a feather to hit me.

The poem "Eight Balloons" can be sung to the tune "Twinkle, Twinkle Little Star." Sing the melody completely through three times for poem lines 1–12, then repeat the melody's last line for poem lines 13–16.

For best results, tape record these songs ahead of time. You may want to enlist the help of your school's music teacher in locating the music.

Activity 11: Contractions

Poem:

    "Homework Machine," page 56

Read the poem and then brainstorm with your class what it would be like to have such a machine at their disposal. Give students time to design a homework machine of their own and describe how it would work. You may want to demonstrate a pre-made machine to give the children an idea on how to get started (this, of course, depends on the grade level). Start by cutting two slits in an empty shoe box, one at the top of the box marked "input" and one at the bottom marked "output." Decorate the box with knobs, buttons, bulbs, etc. Inside the shoe box construct a little cardboard pathway by taking off the cover of the shoe box. This will allow the small card to fall down the pathway from the "input" hole to the "output" hole. In the process, the little card flips over automatically, revealing the answer to the problem. On one side of the card, write a contraction, on the reverse side write the two words for that contraction. (See diagram on next page.)

To play the "Homework Machine" game, set a pile of contraction cards next to the machine. Let each player in turn choose a card, read the contraction, and give the two words for that contraction. He or she then can insert the card into the "input" slot and check the answer when it comes out. Players keep their own score, counting the correct responses.

You may want to extend this activity to inventing other machines that could do jobs that we don't like to do or that would save time, money, or energy. An example might be a bed-making machine, a robot room cleaner, or a dirty clothes vacuum cleaner. This can serve as a good creative writing project or as an introduction to a social studies unit on inventors and inventions. As a supplement, check your school or local library for the *Invention Book* by Steven Caney.

The following contractions are appropriate for the "Homework Machine" game:

are not	aren't	she will	she'll
cannot	can't	should not	shouldn't
could not	couldn't	that is	that's
do not	don't	there is	there's
does not	doesn't	they have	they've
had not	hadn't	they will	they'll
has not	hasn't	was not	wasn't
he had, he would	he'd	we are	we're
he is, he has	he's	we had, we would	we'd
he will	he'll	we have	we've
here is	here's	we will	we'll
I am	I'm	were not	weren't
I had, I would	I'd	who is	who's
I have	I've	what is	what's
I will	I'll	will not	won't

is not	isn't	would not	wouldn't
let us	let's	you are	you're
shall not	shan't	you had, you would	you'd
she is, she has	she's	you have	you've
she had, she would	she'd	you will	you'll

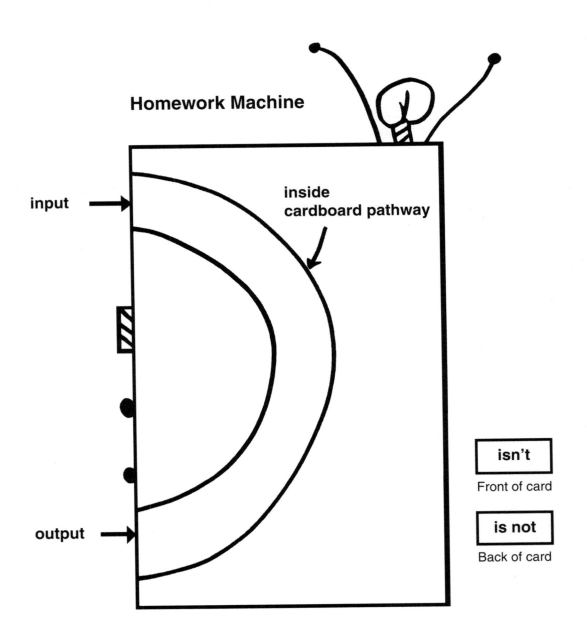

Homework Machine

input

inside
cardboard pathway

output

isn't
Front of card

is not
Back of card

Activity 12: Self-esteem

Poem:
"Adventures of a Frisbee," page 70

Read the poem and discuss all the things that the Frisbee wished it could be. Let this be an opportunity for students to think about and describe things they wish they could do or people they would like to be like, and why. Of course, as the Frisbee "rolled home, quite glad to be a Frisbee once again," the discussion should encourage your students to be glad about who they are, too. Each person has special talents and strengths different from anyone else. One activity may be to have your students list as many positive traits, abilities, or good things about themselves as they can. Have them write this list into paragraph form, omitting their name. Collect the descriptions, mix them up, and pass them out randomly to the class. Ask each student to read the paragraph they've received and see if they know which classmate it describes. Permit them to go to that classmate and see if they were correct. If not, let them try again until the writer is identified.

As a different activity, instruct each person to write down something positive about each member of the class, to be read only by the individual it was written for. This develops a more positive classroom climate by building each other up.

Try turning "Adventures of a Frisbee" into a play with dialogue and narration that can be acted out by students or puppets. Brainstorm as a class a play that might use animals who wish to be something else but come to realize that they can do certain things better than any other animal and thus should do their best at being themselves.

Activity 13: Categorization

Poem:
"Bear in There," page 47

One way to enjoy a reading of this poem is to discuss its action verbs: *nibbling, munching, slurping,* and *licking.* Make a list of more action words that have to do with eating, such as *sipping, smacking,* or *crunching.* This activity could extend into a class-written poem using the rhyming pattern of "Bear in There."

Another fun activity for students is to make a game or contest of categorizing foods in a variety of ways, such as,

1. Food types (vegetables, fruits, meat)
2. Colors or shapes of food
3. Foods stored in the refrigerator
4. Foods that need to be cooked

To extend this activity further, encourage your children to draw pictures of these different foods or cut them out of old magazines (including garden and seed catalogs) and put them on 3x5 index cards. With these they can practice putting their cards in alphabetical order.

As a whole group brainstorming session, list as many foods under each letter of the alphabet as possible. Children will enjoy compiling their efforts into a classroom book titled *Foods From A to Z.*

For additional reading enjoyment on the subject of food, introduce the children to two books by Robert Munsch—*Something Good* and *Moira's Birthday.*

Activity 14: Propaganda/Persuasion Techniques

Poem:

"Clarence," page 154

This poem lends itself to a great discussion on the propaganda/persuasion techniques used in TV commercials and newspaper advertisements. (Did you know it's propaganda if it's used against you; it's persuasion if it's used by you?) A list of these techniques and some examples follow:

Name calling—using negative or derogatory words, such as "not as strong as" or "weaker than" to convince consumers that another product is inferior.

Glittering generality—using a generalized statement, but making it sound like fact, as in "Many people use . . ." How many is "many?"

Card stacking—telling the facts from one side only.

Testimonials—using the testimony of someone consumers respect or admire.

Bandwagon—using the argument that "Everybody's buying it, so don't be left out."

Plain folks—saying that people just like you are buying it, so why don't you?

Red herring—highlighting a minor detail to draw you away from more important issues.

Exigency—giving the impression that you must act quickly in order to take advantage of the opportunity.

Transfer—trying to transfer your feelings about one thing to another, such as by using cute puppies in a soft drink ad.

Innuendo—giving an impression or hinting that something is being kept hidden.

Snob appeal—making you feel you're among the rich, popular, or elite if you use this product.

Flag waving—connecting the use of the product with patriotic or American ideals.

Hidden fears—trying to scare you into using a product.

Facts and figures—using statistics and percentages to convince you of the product's worth.

Buzz words—using words that are popular at the time, like *all-natural, recyclable,* etc.

The following activities and ideas can enhance the study of propaganda/persuasion techniques:

1. Using old magazines, have students take out pages that illustrate advertisements and decide which technique is being used. Compile these into a book or display them on a bulletin board.

2. Students can choose a local business or real product to write an advertisement for.

3. Students may wish to create their own product and ad campaign to sell their product. Videotape the children sharing these with the class.

4. You can videotape a series of commercials on TV for students to analyze and name the technique being used.

Have your students try a little friendly persuasion themselves! Ask them if they've ever tried to convince their sister or brother to do something for them. What tone of voice or facial expressions did they use? When persuading parents to let them go somewhere with their friends, what approaches worked best? Do students use a different tone of voice when talking with parents? What words or phrases work best? Does the time and setting make a difference when approaching certain family members? In what ways do fatigue or moodiness make a difference in parent responses?

Have your students write a short commercial on one of the following situations:

- persuading your parents to increase your weekly allowance
- convincing your teacher to cancel homework for one night
- persuading your sister or brother to baby sit so you can go out
- talking your parents into letting you get a new pet
- persuading your parents to teach you how to drive a car
- getting your sister or brother to clean your room
- sweet-talking your sister or brother into sharing some Halloween candy with you

To adapt this activity to the primary level, you may want to videotape commercials from the Saturday morning children's programming. There you will find a variety of commercials on children's toys, candy, and foods. After watching the videotape with the students, ask them if they've bought (or asked their parents to buy) the things they've seen on TV commercials. Make a list of all the items the students name. Ask them why they wanted to buy these products. What did the commercial do or say that made them want the product?

Students may wish to find examples of persuasion in printed material, such as the local newspaper or various children's magazines such as *3•2•1 Contact, Boy's Life, Sports Illustrated for Kids*, and *Odyssey*.

Activity 15: Tongue Twisters—Figures of Speech

Poem:

"Poemsicle," page 133

Ask for volunteers to read this poem out loud. Children enjoy hearing others read this lengthy tongue twister! Encourage your students to research the library for poetry and riddle books containing tongue twisters. Compile a loose-leaf classroom anthology in which students illustrate the tongue twisters they've found or written themselves. You might even involve the school art teacher in drawing illustrations for the cover and tongue twisters included in the book. The finished product can be displayed in the school library for all the students to enjoy!

The study of tongue twisters would fit well with language lessons on figures of speech. First start with *alliteration,* which is the repetition of the same initial letter, sound, or group of sounds in a series of words. Here are some examples:

"A Moose"

A *moose* and his *mate munched* a *melon.*
They finished and *meandered* about smellin'
For *more morsels* to eat,
They *managed* a treat
of *mashed* potatoes a farmer was sellin'.

"Tara Tucker"

Tara Tucker tickled her brother.
He *tried to tickle* her back.
But *Tara Tucker tickled* her brother
Till he *tumbled* and fell on a *tack.*

"Sliding"

Ice is *so slippery* and *smooth,* you *see,*
And *snow* is *so soft* and nice.
I *slid* on my *sled*
But *slipped* off it instead.
And *skated* face first on the ice.

Extend your lesson by including *onomatopoeia,* which is the use of a word to describe or imitate a natural sound or the sound made by an object or an action. Shel Silverstein's poem "Squishy Touch" is a perfect example of this figure of speech.

Personification is a figure of speech in which human characteristics are given to an animal, plant, element of nature, object, etc. Shel Sivlerstein's poem "Catching" is an effective example of this figure of speech (A head cold trying to elude being caught.).

Hyperbole is an exaggeration that is so dramatic that no one would believe the statement is true. A couple of examples follow:

"The Vegetable Tray"

Every evening before supper
My mother will busily say,
"Please cut up the broccoli and celery
For our daily vegetable tray."
I cut and dice, and chop and slice
The carrots and asparagus spears.
But when I cut the onions in two,
I cry a bucket of tears.

A *simile* is a figure of speech using the words "like" or "as" to compare one object or idea with another to suggest that they are alike. Such as:

"The Bunny"

Have you ever seen a bunny
With a shiny, wiggly nose?
It's so cute and hoppy
And friendly, I suppose.
The funniest part of a bunny
Is the soft, round, tail of fluff.
For it really looks just *like my mom's*
Talcum powder puff.

A *metaphor* is a comparison of one thing or idea to another which is not normally related. Such as the following poem:

"Love"

When I saw your face
My heart went "flutter"
'Cuz *you stuck to my ribs*
Like peanut butter.
I saw your face
With that big, broad smile.
Those pumpkin teeth
Should last awhile.
Your hair is long
And pretty curly.
It makes you look
A little squirrely.
The cute little ears
On the side of your face
Look like donuts
That are out of place.
Your nose is funny
The way it sits.
It seems to be covered
With tiny zits!
Your body appears
To be tall and lean,
A perfect replica
Of a green string bean.
Your outrageous looks
Don't really matter,
For my heart still goes
"Pitter-patter."

Activity 16: The Challenged Individual

Poem:

"Deaf Donald," page 143

This poem offers an obvious introduction to discussing the different learning and physical conditions faced by the challenged students who are mainstreamed into our classrooms. Using the blackboard or chart paper, brainstorm and list physical conditions that are noticeable and unnoticeable at a glance, such as the following:

Noticeable Physical Differences	*Unnoticeable Physical Differences*
Mental challenges (some)	Mental challenges
Cerebral palsy	Deafness
Blindness	Learning impairments
Loss of limbs	Emotional disturbances
Paraplegia	

Discuss these different conditions honestly and openly with your students, making it clear that though some people may be physically impaired, they also may have areas of great skill or strength. Students will be more understanding if they realize that we all have areas of weakness as well as things we may excel in. This is an appropriate time for students to list their own strengths and weaknesses or "differences" on a sheet of paper. Encourage them to improve those skills that are weak and be willing to help others with their strengths, abilities, and talents. Emphasize that they should never ridicule or make fun of those who are different. This topic should be handled as sensitively as possible, making sure students understand their role in showing support and compassion toward their challenged classmates, neighbors, etc.

An activity students will enjoy together is learning how to finger spell using the American Sign Language alphabet. More literature on communicating with the deaf can be obtained through the National Technical Institute for the Deaf (One Lomb Memorial Drive, P.O. Box 9887, Rochester, NY 14623-0887). Students may find the Braille alphabet and numbers chart interesting and fun to learn as well. Contact your school or district's special education department to get copies of these materials to share with your students.

Unimpaired students will become more sensitive to the needs of the challenged individual by involving them in some simulation activities. For example, many mentally challenged people (those with subaverage intellectual functioning and adaptive behavior problems) take longer to do things, and tasks are more difficult for them, so they must try harder. Try the following to illustrate their day-to-day challenges:

1. Assign your students to write one or two sentences composed of words having two syllables.

2. Prepare a list of directions, such as stand up, sit down, turn around, pat your head, clap three times, snap your fingers once, stamp your feet twice, face the back of the room, etc. Tell the children you are going to give them the directions only once. Read the directions quickly, then tell them to begin. Allow the children to do as much as they can, then ask them what would make the task easier. You will get responses such as slow down, write the

directions on the board, let us practice, let us say the directions with you, let us learn three or four then add more, etc. List these suggestions on the board, then try them.

3. Pair each student up with a partner. Tell one partner in each pair to think of a shape, but not say it out loud. With partners sitting back to back, instruct the first partner to tell the second how to draw the shape without saying its name.

A learning impairment, a disorder in one or more basic psychological/cognitive processes, may manifest itself in an imperfect ability to listen, speak, read, write, spell, or do mathematical calculations. Here are some simulation activities (these tasks alter the students' perception or expectations of what is read or being written):

1. Have students hold a piece of paper to their foreheads and write on it, without looking, the numbers 1 to 10, so they can be read from left to right when completed.

2. Tell students to hold a piece of paper with a message on it in front of a mirror and try to read it.

3. Have students look into a mirror and try to draw or write on a paper that is in front of them.

To simulate a visual impairment, try the following activities:

1. Show your students a film or cartoon out of focus to simulate legal blindness (vision 20/70 or less in the better eye with correction). Show the film again with the picture in focus.

2. Play only the audio track of an unfamiliar film or cartoon (darken the picture completely or cover the lens) to simulate total blindness. Have the students describe the film's scenery, characters, colors, and action. Repeat the film with the picture intact. Was it as they expected?

Here are some deafness and hearing loss simulation activities:

1. Divide students into pairs or small groups. Using facial expressions, body language, and hand gestures only (no verbal speech), have students try to communicate simple phrases; for example, time for lunch, I want a drink, I want to go home, I hate homework, I'm glad to see you, I like you, it's raining outside, my teacher is nice. Compare the different ways to communicate the same phrase.

2. Show a film with the sound low and with other competing sounds, such as a cassette, TV, or radio playing, students playing outside, or traffic noise.

3. Turn on a radio or record player. Ask students if they can feel the vibrations when they touch it. from the table it is on? on the floor beneath it?

People with cerebral palsy or motor coordination problems often do not have control of their muscles, or their muscles seem stiff or weak. To simulate the lack of muscle control, have students try the following:

1. Lie down on the floor, and try to get up without using their heads.

2. Get tightly wrapped in a blanket, and try to roll over.

3. Put a pair of thick socks on each hand or have all their fingers except their thumbs taped down. Try to tie shoes, button up a shirt, eat lunch, or reach into a bag and try to identify familiar objects.

Some further follow-up on this topic is to discuss and research some famous learning and physically challenged individuals who have made lasting contributions to society or shown great courage in overcoming their difficulties. Examples are Helen Keller, Stevie Wonder, Woodrow

Wilson, Hans Christian Andersen, Bruce Jenner, Albert Einstein, Stephen Hawkins, Juliette Low, Thomas Edison, Winston Churchill, Nelson Rockefeller, Whoopi Goldberg, Leonardo da Vinci, General George Patton, Greg Louganis, and Cher. Students need to know that, they too, can rise above their physical and learning difficulties and become worthwhile people, even if they don't make visible, long-lasting contributions.

Activity 17: Dictionary Skills/Riddle Writing

Poem:

"What Did?" page 16

Read this poem to the class and see if they understand the nature of riddles. Encourage your students to experiment with language and come up with their own riddles. Use your dictionary, mix up some vocabulary words, add a little silliness, and you have a new approach to language arts! This activity can be done as a whole class, in a small group, with parents, or individually. Follow the steps to this riddle recipe and motivate your students, beyond words! (This riddle recipe has been used with permission from Mike Thaler, America's "Riddle King.")

Step 1—Pick a subject. The subject can be anything. You can create riddles about mice, cats, chairs, or stars. The sky's the limit! Let's pick pigs.

Step 2—Make up a list of words that mean the same as your subject (synonyms) and words closely related to your subject. For pigs, consider where they live, noises they make, and food products. A sample list might include *hog, boar, oink, bacon, ham, mud, pork, swine, pen, sty, sow, grunt,* and *slop.* A dictionary, a thesaurus, an encyclopedia, and a book on farm animals will help a lot.

Step 3—Pick any word on your list and drop the first letter. Take away the *h* from *ham,* and you get *am.*

Step 4—Make a list of words that begin with what's left. A dictionary makes this easy. You'll find words like *amateur, America, ambulance, amnesia,* and *Amsterdam.*

Step 5—(the magic part) Put back the letter you dropped on each of the words. Now you've got *hamateur, Hamerica, hambulance, hamnesia,* and *Hamsterdam.*

Step 6—Make up your riddle questions, using relevant facts from the definitions of the real words. What do you call a pig that's not a professional? *A hamateur.* What country has the most free pigs? *Hamerica.* How do you take a pig to the hospital? *In a hambulance.* What do you call it when a pig loses its memory? *Hamnesia.* What is the pig's favorite city in Holland? *Hamsterdam.*

It's as simple as that. There is, however, one problem you may encounter. On a few words, if you drop the first letter, there's nothing to work with. Take away the *s* from the word *snout* and you get *nout.* There are just "nout" any words in the dictionary that begin with n-o-u-t. If this happens, drop the second letter also. Take away the *n* from *nout* and you get *out.* Lots of words and phrases begin with out: *outlaw, outstanding, outfit, outer space.* Now just put the *sn* back on. See what you get? *Snoutlaw, snoutstanding, snoutfit, snouter space.*

What do you call a pig who robs banks? *A snoutlaw.*

What do you call a pig who gets straight A's? *Snoutstanding!*

What do you call a pig's new clothes? *Its snoutfit.*

Where do pig astronauts travel? *In snouter space.*

43

One last tip: When kids have reached Step 3, they may find it easiest to pick one-syllable words, at least until they've made a few riddles and can begin to see which words have the most potential.

Using this simple riddle-writing process, your students can create thousands of riddles. They can expand their vocabulary and general knowledge, and enhance their writing and thinking skills. They can use reference books, learn synonyms, and best of all, have fun with language and achieve success and joy by using it.

Try expanding this lesson into a school-wide riddle-writing contest! Make a copy of the form on the following page for each teacher in your building, Grades 2–5.

RIDDLE-WRITING CONTEST COUPON

Teacher's name:_____Date: _____

Student's name:_____Grade: _____

Riddle entry: _____

_____

_____

Riddles are due by: _____

Contest coupons are to be submitted to: _____

This contest is sponsored by: _____

All riddles are to be original, not copied from books.

RIDDLE-WRITING CONTEST COUPON

Teacher's name:_____Date: _____

Student's name:_____Grade: _____

Riddle entry: _____

_____

_____

Riddles are due by: _____

Contest coupons are to be submitted to: _____

This contest is sponsored by: _____

All riddles are to be original, not copied from books.

Activity 18: Idioms

Poems:

    "Catching," page 142

    "The Sitter," page 14

An idiom is an expression (group of words) whose meaning is not predictable from the meanings or arrangement of the individual words. For example, "It's raining cats and dogs."

After reading "The Sitter" and "Catching," discuss the definition of idioms with your students. Brainstorm a list and record them on chart paper. Choose an idiom such as "Cat got your tongue?" and ask students what kind of picture pops into their heads. Then discuss what the expression really means. Students may be unfamiliar with the meanings of other idioms on the list. Be prepared to explain and discuss these together.

To carry this activity further, ask your students to illustrate an idiomatic phrase without writing it on their paper. Then ask each child in turn to show the picture to the class and let others try to guess the idiom depicted. Compile the finished illustrations into a classroom book.

Two fictional characters that take idiomatic phrases literally and act on them are Amelia Bedelia and Deputy Dan. Peggy Parish has written many books about Amelia Bedelia, including *Amelia Bedelia and the Surprise Shower; Come Back, Amelia Bedelia;* and *Play Ball, Amelia Bedelia.* Joseph Rosenbloom created *Deputy Dan and the Bank Robbers* and *Deputy Dan Gets His Man,* which have wonderfully funny illustrations by Tim Raglin. Your students will enjoy the crazy antics of these two characters so much that it will seem Amelia Bedelia and Deputy Dan should meet each other. Discuss the particular idioms that these characters take literally in the stories. Encourage your children to write a story about how Deputy Dan and Amelia Bedelia meet each other and become friends (or get married). Give children opportunities to share these stories with each other.

The following list of idioms may help with your activities:

back off	last straw
beat his brains out	money to burn
beat it	off your rocker
blow the whistle on her	on cloud nine
break a record	on pins and needles
break the ice	out in left field
bring home the bacon	out of sight
butterflies in my stomach	pulling your leg
catch a cold	quit cold turkey
chip on the shoulder	ran out of steam
clear as mud	right up your alley
cut it out	rip off
don't bug me	running behind
down in the dumps	see eye to eye

down the drain
drop me a line
eat your words
fit as a fiddle
flying high
full of baloney
get off my back
go fly a kite
go jump in the lake
green thumb
horsing around
it's in the bag

shake a leg
skin of his teeth
stop on a dime
the pits
time flies
under the weather
up in the air
use your noodle
we're in hot water
we're in the same boat
your name will be mud
zero in on

For further fun, Myra Shulman Auslin has written six workbooks explaining and teaching children about idioms: *Raining Cats and Dogs, Holding Your Horses, Monkey Business, Sticky Fingers, Back Off,* and *In the Doghouse.* They may be ordered from Dormac, Inc. (P.O. Box 1699, Beaverton, OR 97075-1699).

Part Three

Miscellaneous Books

Activity 19: Mother's Day/Father's Day

Book:

The Giving Tree

When Shel Silverstein wrote this book in 1964, he described it as merely a relationship between two people, "one gives and the other takes." Interestingly, many readers see things differently—pastors call it a parable on the "joys of giving," mothers see themselves as the tree, giving without expecting anything in return. Though the interpretations are varied, this book nonetheless seems to touch a sensitive chord in all of us.

What a perfect opportunity to write a loving, sensitive story for a Mother's or Father's Day gift. After reading *The Giving Tree* to your class, ask the children to substitute a parent, grandparent, or guardian's name for the tree and write their version of the story. Encourage them to write about the "giver" in their family. Your students may want to write a story short enough to fit inside a card or long enough to be a book with illustrations. If they need more ideas or help, read the story *Love You Forever* by Robert Munsch.

Extend this writing activity into a discussion on the concept of giving and receiving. Discuss Christmas, Hanukkah, or other cultural/religious holidays and how children receive many gifts from their family members. Ask them if they enjoyed "giving" gifts as much as "receiving" them. How many children took time to make gifts for their family and friends? What were they? Brainstorm and list the types of things one could "give" to others, such as participating in a canned food drive, singing to or visiting patients in nursing homes, taking a card to a sick friend, etc. Discuss with your students how these acts of "giving" can occur anytime throughout the year, not just for birthdays or special events.

Activity 20: Synonyms, Antonyms, Homonyms

Book:

Lafcadio, the Lion Who Shot Back

Children will enjoy listening to you read this book. Make the story come alive by creating voices for the various characters. This story lends itself to the study of homonyms, especially as the very first page begins preparing you for the lion's tail (or is it tale?). However, it's difficult to study Homer without meeting his brother and sister also. Prepare to introduce your students to the Nym family by decorating your bulletin board as follows:

Simon–Nym

synonym *(happy, glad)*
Words that mean the same or almost the same.

Antonia–Nym

antonym *(night, day)*
Words that mean the opposite.

Homer–Nym

homonym *(week, weak)*
Words that sound the same, but are spelled differently.

Make an enlarged copy of each Nym face and attach each to an envelope. Secure the envelopes to your bulletin board and create a game for your students. Prepare word cards with pairs of synonyms, antonyms, or homonyms written on them. Code the back of each with a small letter *s, a,* or *h* so the game will be self-correcting. Assign small groups or individuals to play this game during free time or when children have completed their assigned work.

A list of synonyms, antonyms, and homonyms follows for use in making this game.

Synonyms	*Antonyms*	*Homonyms*
all, every	all, none	ate, eight
add, sum	answer, question	bare, bear
ask, question	asked, told	be, bee
below, under	birth, death	beat, beet
car, auto	boy, girl	berry, bury
city, town	close, open	brake, break
damp, wet	come, go	buy, by, bye
end, finish	end, begin	capital, capitol
find, locate	even, odd	cell, sell
go, leave	found, lost	cent, sent, scent
hard, difficult	hard, soft	chews, choose
kind, nice	he, she	chord, cord
large, big	high, low	close, clothes
like, enjoy	his, her	creak, creek

little, small

look, see

make, do

near, close

need, want

new, fresh

night, evening

one, single

place, put

right, correct

run, trot

sound, noise

start, begin

still, silent

take, grab

yell, shout

in, out

kind, cruel

left, right

light, dark

man, woman

many, few

more, less

near, far

no, yes

old, young

on, off

right, wrong

small, large

to, from

up, down

white, black

dear, deer

dew, do, due

ewe, you

fair, fare

fir, fur

flew, flu

flour, flower

for, four, fore

groan, grown

hair, hare

hear, here

heard, herd

heel, heal

I'll, aisle

knew, new, gnu

one, won

Activity 21: CVC Word Patterns

Book:

The Missing Piece

After reading this book, show your children how to play "The Missing Piece" game. Using the patterns below, trace and cut out 16 circles and missing pieces. On each circle, print a consonant; on each missing piece, print a vowel and consonant. The object of the game is to match the correct missing piece to the circle and complete the short-vowel word. This game may be played individually for practice or in a small group setting. Spread the pieces out on a flat surface, encouraging children to work cooperatively to match the missing pieces to the various circles. Make a copy of *The Missing Piece* book cover and glue it to the front of a manila envelope for storing the pieces of this game. (This approach can be adapted to math facts as well.)

The following list shows combinations appropriate for this activity:

Circles	Missing Pieces
b	ed
c	at
d	ip
f	an
g	un
h	im
j	et
k	id
l	ap
m	en
n	ot
p	od
r	ub
s	ad
t	op
w	in

Activity 22: Root Words/Suffixes

Book:

The Missing Piece Meets the Big O

Read this book aloud to your students to prepare them for a game of the same name.

To make this game, cut out eight Missing Piece shapes labeled with one of the following suffixes: *ing, ly, ness, less, ed, en, er, ful.* Make several Big O shapes labeled with one root word on each. (Adjust the root words to fit your grade level.)

To play the game, students will need a score sheet and pencil. Turn the Big O (root word) cards face down. The first player turns over a Big O card, reads the root word, and then tries to find how many Missing Piece (suffix ending) cards make sense with that root word. Players tally on their score sheets each new word they make. Each child takes a turn until the pile of Big O cards is used up. Students then count their tally marks, and the highest score wins.

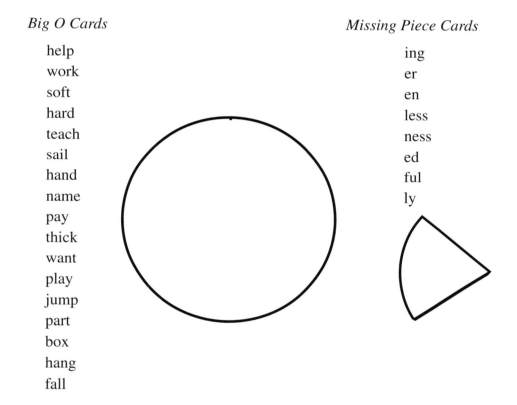

Big O Cards	*Missing Piece Cards*
help	ing
work	er
soft	en
hard	less
teach	ness
sail	ed
hand	ful
name	ly
pay	
thick	
want	
play	
jump	
part	
box	
hang	
fall	

54

Activity 23: Syllabication

> *Book:*
>
> *Who Wants a Cheap Rhinoceros?*

After reading this book, you can't help falling in love with Silverstein's cute rhinoceros! Unfortunately, Shel didn't give this lovable creature a name. For this activity, however, we will refer to him as "Ronnie."

One of the most disliked skill areas that teachers have to cover with elementary students is syllabication! A painless way to teach this skill is a game called "Sylla-Maze." First, make a deck of cards with one-, two-, three-, four-, or more syllable words, one on each card. Make sure one of the word cards says *Ronnie,* for whoever picks this card gets an extra turn. Next, make several "penalty cards" to mix in the deck ("Lose a turn," "Move back two spaces," etc.). Use a pathway game board and decorate it with pictures of "Ronnie."

To begin the game, each player chooses a marker and places it on start. Lay the all the cards face down on the game board. The first player picks a card, reads the word, counts the syllables, and moves that many spaces on the pathway. If students pick a penalty card, they do as it says and play continues. If someone picks a "Ronnie" card, they move two spaces ahead, plus get another turn. Students must get the exact number to finish the game.

Word/penalty cards

allowance	comfortable	hanger	snack
bath	comics	house	terrific
battleship	crooks	imitating	unsinkable
beach	donuts	lap	Lose 1 turn.
cheap	especially	parents	Move ahead three spaces.
coat sale	friendly	rhinoceros	Move back one space.
collecting	grandmother	"Ronnie"	Move back two spaces.
			Return to start.

Here are a few syllabication rules to remind your students of during this skill review:

Rule 1—VCV. If a consonant is between two vowels, it usually goes with the second syllable unless the first vowel is short. Example: *sha-ken, com-ic.*

Rule 2—VCCV. When two consonants are together, divide the word between them unless they are blends or digraphs. Example: *but-ter, pic-ture, push-er.*

Rule 3—VCCCV. When three consonants occur together, divide between the blend or the digraph and the other consonant. Example: *stran-gler.*

Rule 4—Compound. Always divide compound words at the point where the words join. Example: *blue-bird.*

For a more complete list of syllabication rules, refer to *The Reading Teacher's Book of Lists* (Fry, Polk, and Fountoukidis, 1984).

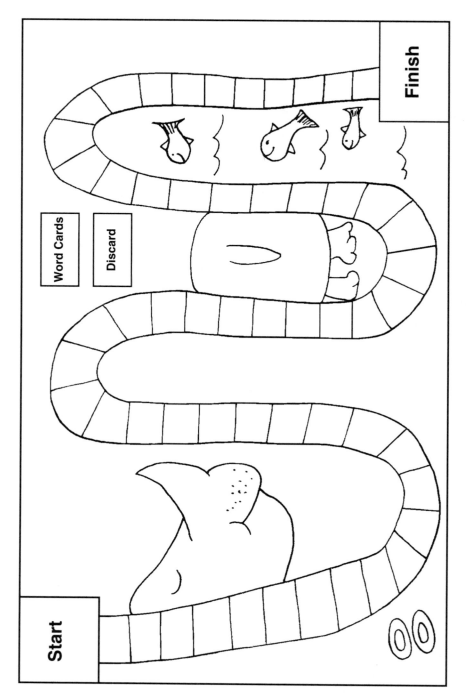

"Sylla Maze"

As an evaluative tool on syllabication, make a puppet or use an existing one and glue the top and bottom of a thin piece of ribbon to the center back of its mouth. You may want to name the puppet "Sylla-Gorilla," "Sylla-Ronnie" (after attaching a cone-shaped horn to his face), or some other "sylla" name. Instruct children individually to insert a word card into the puppet's mouth, sliding it into a position where the thin ribbon would correctly divide the word into syllables. Observe your students' progress and decide if more practice is needed or the skill has been mastered satisfactorily.

Activity 24: Story Participation

Book:

A Giraffe and a Half

Children will enjoy participating in the reading of this Shel Silverstein book. Before you begin, explain to your students they will need to be the sound effects while you read the book. Each time they hear you read the following animals, they are to make the following sound effects:

Rat:	Squeak, squeak!
Bee:	Buzz, buzz!
Snake:	Sssssssssssss!
Skunk	Pew!
Dragon:	Pretend to breathe out fire
Whale:	Splash!

Be sure to practice all the sound effects before beginning the story. Children tend to listen more closely knowing they are a part of the story reading. Read the story at a moderate speed and purposely hesitate on the animal words so students will catch their cues.

Depending on the grade level, encourage your students to find other books that can be used with sound effects as a story participation piece. You may also have some creative writers who would like to experiment on their own. The following short story (of unknown origin) is a sample.

"The Story of Falling Rock"

Sound effects:

Falling Rock:	Ker plunk!
Running River:	Babble, babble
Little Big Bear:	Grrrr!
Chief:	Ugh!
Found/find:	Ah ha!

There once was an Indian *chief* who had three sons: *Running River, Little Big Bear,* and *Falling Rock.* When his sons became of age, it was necessary for the *chief* to send them out into the world to *find* what they considered the most beautiful thing in the world. *Running River, Little Big Bear,* and *Falling Rock* left their father the *chief* and their tribe for the search. Many moons passed before the sons returned, as they were looking high and low to *find* the most beautiful object.

Finally, *Running River* returned and showed his father the *chief* the most beautiful daisy ever *found.* After many more moons had gone by, *Little Big Bear* returned with the news that the most beautiful object he could *find* was a beautiful sunset. More moons passed, but there was no sign of *Falling Rock.* Finally, the *chief, Running River,* and *Little Big Bear* grew worried over what was taking him so long. In fact, *Falling Rock* never came back. That is why, to this day, when you drive along a highway, you will see signs saying, "Watch for *Falling Rock!*"

Bibliography

Cameron, Polly. *"I Can't" Said the Ant*. New York: Scholastic, 1961.

Caney, Steven. *Invention Book*. New York: Workman, 1985.

Clymer, Eleanor. *Funny Poems*. New York: Scholastic, 1961.

Cowley, Joy. *Ten Loopy Caterpillars*. Miami: P.S.I. & Associates, 1985.

Demurs, Jan. *On Sunday I Lost My Cat*. Worthington, Ohio: Willowisp, Inc. 1986.

Emberley, Barbara. *Drummer Hoff*. New York: Simon & Schuster, 1967.

Fry, Edward; Polk, Jacqueline; and Fountoukidis, Dona. *The Reading Teacher's Book of Lists*. Englewood Cliffs, NJ: Prentice-Hall, 1984.

Hollinger, Ray. *Games Teachers Make*. Willow Street, PA: Instructional Design Associates, 1979.

Keller, Charles. *Tongue Twisters*. New York: Simon & Schuster, 1989.

Kellogg, Steven. *Paul Bunyan*. New York: William Morrow, 1984.

———. *Pecos Bill*. New York: William Morrow, 1986.

Moss, Jeff. *The Butterfly Jar*. New York: Bantam Books, 1989.

———. *The Other Side of the Door*. New York: Bantam Books, 1991.

Munsch, Robert. *Love You Forever*. Willowdale, Ontario, Canada: Firefly Books, 1989.

———. *Moira's Birthday*. Willowdale, Ontario, Canada: Annick Press, 1989.

———. *Something Good*. Willowdale, Ontario, Canada: Annick Press, 1990.

New York State Office of Mental Retardation and Developmental Disabilities. "The Kids Project" (booklet). (44 Holland Ave., Albany, New York 12229).

Parish, Peggy. *Amelia Bedelia and the Surprise Shower*. New York: Harper & Row, 1966.

———. *Come Back, Amelia Bedelia*. New York: Harper & Row, 1971.

———. *Play Ball, Amelia Bedelia*. New York: Harper & Row, 1972.

Prelutsky, Jack. *Zoo Doings*. New York: Trumpet, 1983.

Rosenbloom, Joseph. *Deputy Dan and the Bank Robbers*. New York: Random House, 1985.

———. *Deputy Dan Gets His Man*. New York: Random House, 1985.

Sardella, Donna, and Pierce, Mary. "The Kids Project." (program) Syracuse, NY: Syracuse Developmental Center, 1978

Sendak, Maurice. *Chicken Soup With Rice*. New York: Scholastic, 1962.

Silverstein, Shel. *A Giraffe and a Half*. New York: Harper & Row, 1964.

———. *The Giving Tree*. New York: Harper & Row, 1964.

———. *Lafcadio, the Lion Who Shot Back*. New York: Harper & Row, 1963.

———. *A Light in the Attic*. New York: Harper & Row, 1981.

———. *The Missing Piece*. New York: Harper & Row, 1976.

———. *The Missing Piece Meets the Big O*. New York: Harper & Row, 1981.

———. *Where the Sidewalk Ends*. New York: Harper & Row, 1974.

———. *Who Wants a Cheap Rhinoceros?* New York: Macmillan, 1964.

Thaler, Mike. "The Super-Duper Riddle Recipe." *Instructor Magazine*, Sept.1986: 114–115.

Wiesner, William. *A Rocket in My Pocket*. New York: Scholastic, 1967.

York, Carol Beach. Retold *Ichabod Crane*. Mahwah, NJ: Troll Associates, 1980.

———. Retold *Mike Fink*. Mahwah, NJ: Troll Associates, 1980.

DATE DUE
DATE DE RETOUR

OCT 2 2 2003	
NOV 0 2 2003	
MAR 1 4 2006	
MAR 2 1 2006	
OCT 1 5 2007	
OCT 1 5 2007	